Bikes

This North American edition first published in 1986 by
Gareth Stevens, Inc.
7221 West Green·Tree Road   Milwaukee, Wisconsin 53223, USA
U.S. edition, this format, copyright © 1986
Text and additional illustrations copyright © 1986 by Gareth Stevens, Inc.
Illustrations copyright © 1985 by Frances Lincoln Ltd.

Conceived, designed, and first produced in the United Kingdom with an original text copyright by
Frances Lincoln Ltd.

Library of Congress Cataloging-in-Publication Data

Thompson, Graham, 1940-
  Bikes.

  (Wheels)
  Includes index.
  Summary: Illustrations and simple text introduce the characteristics and uses
of a variety of bicycles including tricycles, unicycles, choppers, and
rickshaws.
  1. Bicycles—Juvenile literature. [1. Bicycles] I.   Title. II. Series: Thompson,
Graham, 1940-
      Wheels.
TL410.T48   1986   796.6   86-5701
                        629.2'272

ISBN 1-55532-099-6
ISBN 1-55532-074-0 (lib. bdg.)

Art direction and design:
      Debbie MacKinnon & Gary Moseley
Additional illustration/design: Laurie Shock

Typeset by: Ries Graphics, ltd.
Series editor: Mark J. Sachner

Bikes

Graham Thompson

Gareth Stevens Publishing
Milwaukee

Tricycle and Bicycle

It is hard to balance on only two wheels. That is why tricycles have three wheels. And that is why this bicycle has training wheels.

4

BMX Bikes

BMX means Bicycle Motocross. A BMX is small, strong, and sturdy. What kind of stunt is number 15 doing?

Racing Bikes and Tandem

Racing bikes are thin and light. The other bike in this picture is a tandem. How are tandems different from racing bikes?

Rickshaw

This rickshaw is a large tricycle. Riding in one might be fun. So might driving one!

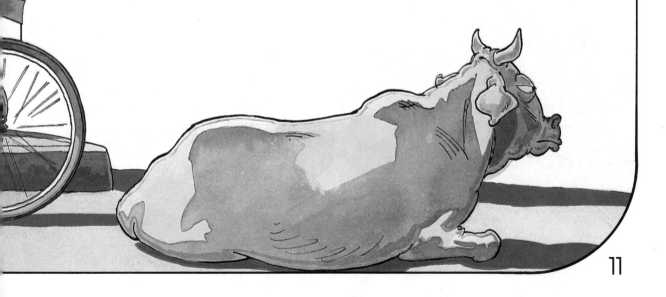

Unicycle

A unicycle has just one wheel. It takes a long time to learn to ride. Where have you seen a unicycle?

13

Standard Motorcycles

Motorcycles have engines and go very fast. Most riders wear helmets to protect their heads if they fall.

Dirt Bikes

Dirt bikes have thick tires. They are also light and springy. They can jump over things and ride in mud.

17

Dirt Track Racing

These motorcycles race on a track. They have light bodies, wide handlebars, and thin tires. They are built for speed!

Sidecar Racing

These bikes are fun to watch. They have two riders. One rider drives, and the other balances the bike around corners.

Chopper

The chopper, or easyrider, has a long front fork. This gives a smoother ride. It also makes the bike look fast.

Index of Bikes